S0-FCL-430

2026
Faith for Today
PLANNER

This planner belongs to:

_____

2026 Faith for Today Planner

Copyright © 2025 Joel Osteen

All rights reserved. No part of this book may be reproduced or transmitted in any form or by any means, electronic or mechanical, including photocopying, recording, or by any information storage and retrieval system, without permission in writing from the publisher.

Scripture quotations are taken from the Holy Bible, New International Version®, NIV®. Copyright © 1973, 1978, 1984, 2011 by Biblica, Inc.™ Used by permission of Zondervan. All rights reserved worldwide. www.zondervan.com The "NIV" and "New International Version" are trademarks registered in the United States Patent and Trademark Office by Biblica, Inc.™

ISBN: 978-1-963492-39-2

Created and assembled for Joel Osteen Ministries by
Breakfast for Seven
breakfastforseven.com

Printed in China.

For additional resources by Joel Osteen, visit JoelOsteen.com.

2026 OVERVIEW & HOLIDAYS

JANUARY
S	M	T	W	T	F	S
				1	2	3
4	5	6	7	8	9	10
11	12	13	14	15	16	17
18	19	20	21	22	23	24
25	26	27	28	29	30	31

FEBRUARY
S	M	T	W	T	F	S
1	2	3	4	5	6	7
8	9	10	11	12	13	14
15	16	17	18	19	20	21
22	23	24	25	26	27	28

MARCH
S	M	T	W	T	F	S
1	2	3	4	5	6	7
8	9	10	11	12	13	14
15	16	17	18	19	20	21
22	23	24	25	26	27	28
29	30	31				

APRIL
S	M	T	W	T	F	S
			1	2	3	4
5	6	7	8	9	10	11
12	13	14	15	16	17	18
19	20	21	22	23	24	25
26	27	28	29	30		

MAY
S	M	T	W	T	F	S
					1	2
3	4	5	6	7	8	9
10	11	12	13	14	15	16
17	18	19	20	21	22	23
24	25	26	27	28	29	30
31						

JUNE
S	M	T	W	T	F	S
	1	2	3	4	5	6
7	8	9	10	11	12	13
14	15	16	17	18	19	20
21	22	23	24	25	26	27
28	29	30				

JULY
S	M	T	W	T	F	S
			1	2	3	4
5	6	7	8	9	10	11
12	13	14	15	16	17	18
19	20	21	22	23	24	25
26	27	28	29	30	31	

AUGUST
S	M	T	W	T	F	S
						1
2	3	4	5	6	7	8
9	10	11	12	13	14	15
16	17	18	19	20	21	22
23	24	25	26	27	28	29
30	31					

SEPTEMBER
S	M	T	W	T	F	S
		1	2	3	4	5
6	7	8	9	10	11	12
13	14	15	16	17	18	19
20	21	22	23	24	25	26
27	28	29	30			

OCTOBER
S	M	T	W	T	F	S
				1	2	3
4	5	6	7	8	9	10
11	12	13	14	15	16	17
18	19	20	21	22	23	24
25	26	27	28	29	30	31

NOVEMBER
S	M	T	W	T	F	S
1	2	3	4	5	6	7
8	9	10	11	12	13	14
15	16	17	18	19	20	21
22	23	24	25	26	27	28
29	30					

DECEMBER
S	M	T	W	T	F	S
		1	2	3	4	5
6	7	8	9	10	11	12
13	14	15	16	17	18	19
20	21	22	23	24	25	26
27	28	29	30	31		

- Jan 1 — New Year's Day
- Jan 19 — Martin Luther King, Jr. Day (USA)
- Feb 12 — Lincoln's Birthday (USA)
- Feb 14 — Valentine's Day
- Feb 16 — Presidents' Day (USA)
- Feb 18 — Ash Wednesday
- Mar 8 — Daylight Saving Time begins
- Mar 17 — St. Patrick's Day
- Mar 20 — Spring begins
- Mar 29 — Palm Sunday
- Apr 3 — Good Friday
- Apr 5 — Easter / Resurrection Sunday
- May 7 — National Day of Prayer
- May 10 — Mother's Day
- May 18 — Victoria Day (CAN)
- May 25 — Memorial Day (USA)
- Jun 19 — Juneteenth (USA)
- Jun 21 — Father's Day
- Jun 21 — Summer begins
- Jul 1 — Canada Day (CAN)
- Jul 4 — Independence Day
- Aug 3 — Civic Day (CAN)
- Sep 7 — Labor Day
- Sep 22 — Fall begins
- Oct 12 — Columbus Day (USA) / Thanksgiving Day (CAN)
- Oct 31 — Halloween
- Nov 1 — Daylight Saving Time ends
- Nov 11 — Veterans Day (USA) / Remembrance Day (CAN)
- Nov 26 — Thanksgiving Day (USA)
- Dec 21 — Winter begins
- Dec 24 — Christmas Eve
- Dec 25 — Christmas Day
- Dec 26 — Boxing Day (CAN)
- Dec 31 — New Year's Eve

2026

I BELIEVE THIS IS YOUR YEAR

FOR BLESSING,

FOR ABUNDANCE,

FOR HOPE,

AND FOR NEW LEVELS OF FAITH.

Faith for Today — 2026

In Acts 14, the apostle Paul noticed a crippled man in the crowd while he was preaching. This man had never walked a day in his life. People around him probably labeled his situation as hopeless and impossible. But Paul could see something in his expression. He realized the man had faith to be healed.

Mid-message, Paul called out, *". . . Stand up on your feet! . . ."* (Acts 14:10). Immediately, the man leaped to his feet and began walking!

What made the difference? *Faith.* This man believed something good was about to happen. And that's what the *2026 Faith for Today Planner* is all about — a daily invitation to live with **faith** for **today**. Not yesterday's disappointments. Not tomorrow's worries. But faith that believes **God is working right now, in this moment, to bring His promises to pass in and around you**.

Yes, we all face challenges. We can find reasons to be discouraged. But this year, don't let disappointment talk you out of what God wants to do. The very fact that you're holding this planner is a reminder that God has a purpose for you — and it's extraordinary.

1 Corinthians 2:9 declares, *". . . What no eye has seen, what no ear has heard, and what no human mind has conceived — the things God has prepared for those who love him."* And Hebrews 11:6 says, *"And without faith it is impossible*

Faith for Today ——————————————————————— 2026

to please God . . ." That scripture isn't just about faith for salvation — it's about *faith for daily living.*

- Faith that expects the unexpected
- Faith that believes doors are opening
- Faith that holds on when nothing seems to be changing

The *2026 Faith for Today Planner* is designed to help you cultivate that kind of faith. Each page has been prayerfully crafted to help you stay focused, grounded, and encouraged as you write, reflect, and declare God's Word.

At the beginning of each month, you'll find a fresh theme — a word to lift your spirit, a scripture to guide your heart, and space to capture your vision.

What are you believing God for? What are you praying about? What needs to be accomplished?

There will also be space for you to **write out practical steps you can take toward your calling.** Because faith isn't passive — it's *active*.

> **Faith isn't passive — it's active.**

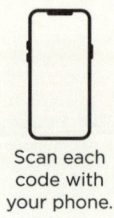

In addition, you'll see a QR code each month — a direct link to a special video or message, designed to keep you uplifted and further increase your faith!

Scan each code with your phone.

Every week, you'll start with a *Faith for Today* **Declaration** — a short, powerful truth you can speak out loud to frame your mindset and shift your atmosphere. Something like, "I'm expecting favor today. I'm stepping into new levels of blessing. God is doing more than I can ask or imagine!"

You'll find weekly prompts as well, designed to help you:

- Write out your to-do's
- Focus your heart in prayer
- Experience God at work in you and through you in the lives of others through a *Faith for Today* Action
- Reflect on where you saw God move during the week — because faith notices and rejoices in the movement of God, whether big or small

Maybe you're praying for a financial breakthrough. Maybe you're working toward a business goal or promotion. Perhaps you're believing for healing like the woman in Mark 5 who had suffered for twelve years. She tried everything she knew to do, and nothing worked — until she heard that Jesus was passing by.

She made up her mind (Mark 5:28): *". . . If I just touch his clothes, I will be healed."* And she was!

At that moment, Jesus didn't just acknowledge her healing — He highlighted her faith. *". . . Daughter, your faith has healed you . . ."* (Mark 5:34).

There were many in the crowd that day, but only one truly touched Him. Why? Because she reached out to Him with faith!

Here's the reality: There will be days when it feels easier to complain, worry, and withdraw. But those are the days when "faith for today" matters most. Paul and Silas experienced this. Imprisoned and in chains, they boldly praised God at midnight. Scripture then says at the sound of their worship, the prison doors flew open and their chains were loosed!

Likewise, you can choose to worship when faced with challenge. And when you do, chains will break. Doors will open. Miracles will happen!

Don't wait for everything to line up to activate your faith. Let your faith go *first*. This planner is your place to do that — one month, one week, and one day at a time.

There may be obstacles this year. The crowd of doubt. The voice of past failures. Negative words that try to talk you out of your dream. But just like the woman who pushed through the crowd to get to Jesus, you can push through every barrier with a made-up mind.

Faith for Today ——————————————————— 2026

No doubt God has whispered dreams into your spirit. So don't let the noise of the world drown them out. Don't let disappointment talk you out of what God still wants to do.

Those hidden dreams that seem too big or too far off to be fulfilled? God put them there. And He is faithful to bring them to pass. This year, don't just brush up against the promises of God — reach out to Him and touch Him with your faith. **Don't merely hope for better days — declare them. Believe for them. Take steps toward them.**

Let this planner be more than a place for appointments and tasks. Let it be a space where you encounter God's presence, declare His promises, and record His faithfulness.

When you live with faith for today, you'll walk in strength. You'll rise in expectation. And you'll see God move in ways you never imagined.

Joel Osteen

Get ready! Your 2026 is full of faith, full of promise, and full of possibility.

This month marks a fresh start, and the new thing God has for you has already begun!

The disappointment or detour that's behind you isn't the end of your story. Even now, God is speaking to your spirit, *"I'm doing a new thing."* That means fresh opportunities, unexpected favor, and open doors are already in motion. But to see the new, you've got to let go of the old. Don't carry yesterday's frustration into today's faith. Boldly choose to get your hopes up. Even if you don't see it yet, trust that God is working behind the scenes. Because He is!

"Forget the former things; do not dwell on the past. See, I am doing a new thing! Now it springs up; do you not perceive it? . . ."
Isaiah 43:18–19

January
AT-A-GLANCE

THIS MONTH, I'M PUTTING MY FAITH IN GOD FOR:

_____
_____
_____
_____
_____
_____

GOALS & DESIRES THIS MONTH:

TO-DO THIS MONTH

- ○ _____
- ○ _____
- ○ _____
- ○ _____
- ○ _____
- ○ _____
- ○ _____

Increase your faith!
Scan now and watch a special message from Pastor Joel!

SUNDAY	MONDAY	TUESDAY	WEDNESDAY
28	29	30	31
4	5	6	7
11	12	13	14
18	19 Martin Luther King, Jr. Day (USA)	20	21
25	26	27	28

January
MONTHLY VIEW

THURSDAY	FRIDAY	SATURDAY
1 New Year's Day	2	3
8	9	10
15	16	17
22	23	24
29	30	31

NOTES

With Jesus, your future only gets brighter!

— Joel

THIS WEEK'S SCRIPTURE:

And without faith it is impossible to please God, because anyone who comes to him must believe that he exists and that he rewards those who earnestly seek him.

HEBREWS 11:6

MY PRAYER THIS WEEK: TO-DO'S:

-
-
-
-
-
-
-
-
-
-

MY *FAITH FOR TODAY* DECLARATION

I am stepping into God's favor. I am anointed, equipped, and positioned for something greater!

January
WEEKLY PLANNING

SUNDAY	MONDAY
28	29

TUESDAY	WEDNESDAY
30	31

THURSDAY	FRIDAY
1	2
New Year's Day	

SATURDAY	*FAITH FOR TODAY* ACTION
3	Who is one person you can encourage or help this week?

THIS WEEK I SAW GOD WORKING . . .

I'M CELEBRATING . . . OR LOOKING FORWARD TO . . .

January
WEEKLY REFLECTION

NOTES

THIS WEEK'S SCRIPTURE:

*Because of the L*ORD*'s great love we are not consumed. . . .*
They are new every morning . . .

LAMENTATIONS 3:22-23

MY PRAYER THIS WEEK: **TO-DO'S:**

- ○
- ○
- ○
- ○
- ○
- ○
- ○
- ○
- ○
- ○

MY *FAITH FOR TODAY* DECLARATION

This year, I receive every new thing God has prepared for me — boldly, confidently, and full of faith.

January
WEEKLY PLANNING

SUNDAY	MONDAY
4	5

TUESDAY	WEDNESDAY
6	7

THURSDAY	FRIDAY
8	9

SATURDAY	*FAITH FOR TODAY* ACTION
10	Pray intentionally for someone else's breakthrough. Ask a friend what they're believing God for this year — and commit to praying over it every day this week.

THIS WEEK I SAW GOD WORKING . . .

I'M CELEBRATING . . . OR LOOKING FORWARD TO . . .

January
WEEKLY REFLECTION

NOTES

THIS WEEK'S SCRIPTURE:

Therefore, if anyone is in Christ, the new creation has come: The old has gone, the new is here!

2 CORINTHIANS 5:17

MY PRAYER THIS WEEK:　　　　　　　　**TO-DO'S:**

- ○ _____
- ○ _____
- ○ _____
- ○ _____
- ○ _____
- ○ _____
- ○ _____
- ○ _____
- ○ _____
- ○ _____

MY *FAITH FOR TODAY* DECLARATION

God's mercy is new today. I am forgiven, favored, and free to move forward.

January
WEEKLY PLANNING

SUNDAY 11	MONDAY 12
TUESDAY 13	WEDNESDAY 14
THURSDAY 15	FRIDAY 16
SATURDAY 17	*FAITH FOR TODAY* ACTION

FAITH FOR TODAY ACTION: Bless someone unexpectedly. Pay for a stranger's coffee, give a generous tip, or drop off a gift card to someone in need. Be someone's answered prayer!

THIS WEEK I SAW GOD WORKING . . .

I'M CELEBRATING . . . OR LOOKING FORWARD TO . . .

January
WEEKLY REFLECTION

NOTES

THIS WEEK'S SCRIPTURE:

Let us hold unswervingly to the hope we profess, for he who promised is faithful.

HEBREWS 10:23

MY PRAYER THIS WEEK:

TO-DO'S:

- ○ _____
- ○ _____
- ○ _____
- ○ _____
- ○ _____
- ○ _____
- ○ _____
- ○ _____
- ○ _____
- ○ _____

MY *FAITH FOR TODAY* DECLARATION

I declare this will be a week of sudden breakthroughs, open doors, and divine surprises, in Jesus' name!

january
WEEKLY PLANNING

SUNDAY	MONDAY
18	19
	Martin Luther King, Jr. Day (USA)

TUESDAY	WEDNESDAY
20	21

THURSDAY	FRIDAY
22	23

SATURDAY	*FAITH FOR TODAY* ACTION
24	Encourage someone going through a tough season. Remind them God isn't finished with their story.

THIS WEEK I SAW GOD WORKING . . .

I'M CELEBRATING . . . OR LOOKING FORWARD TO . . .

January
WEEKLY REFLECTION

NOTES

THIS WEEK'S SCRIPTURE:

. . . Forgetting what is behind and straining toward what is ahead, I press on . . .

PHILIPPIANS 3:13–14

MY PRAYER THIS WEEK:

TO-DO'S:

- ○ _____
- ○ _____
- ○ _____
- ○ _____
- ○ _____
- ○ _____
- ○ _____
- ○ _____
- ○ _____
- ○ _____

MY *FAITH FOR TODAY* DECLARATION

My faith is growing stronger every day. I'm expecting the unexpected, believing for the impossible, and living with purpose!

January
WEEKLY PLANNING

SUNDAY	MONDAY
25	26

TUESDAY	WEDNESDAY
27	28

THURSDAY	FRIDAY
29	30

SATURDAY	*FAITH FOR TODAY* ACTION
31	Share your faith. Post or tell a short story of how God came through for you — and invite someone to church or a Bible study with you.

THIS WEEK I SAW GOD WORKING . . .

I'M CELEBRATING . . . OR LOOKING FORWARD TO . . .

January
WEEKLY REFLECTION

NOTES

God's love isn't superficial or seasonal. It's yours to receive — an unshakable foundation beneath everything you are and do.

When you understand just how good God's love is and receive it, you won't have to chase approval, acceptance, or strive to feel secure. Because you already have the greatest affirmation you'll ever need: **God calls you His own.** His love doesn't change based on how your day goes, how others treat you, or how you feel about yourself. God's love is constant, complete, and the key to living with confidence, peace, and strength.

This month, let that truth settle deep in your heart. As God's child and according to Ephesians 3:17–18, you are rooted in love. And from that place of security, you can live boldly, love freely, and have faith for today.

. . . And I pray that you, being rooted and established in love, may have power, together with all the Lord's holy people, to grasp how wide and long and high and deep is the love of Christ.
Ephesians 3:17–18

February
AT-A-GLANCE

THIS MONTH, I'M PUTTING MY FAITH IN GOD FOR:

_____
_____
_____
_____
_____
_____

GOALS & DESIRES THIS MONTH:

TO-DO THIS MONTH

- _____
- _____
- _____
- _____
- _____
- _____
- _____

Increase your faith!
Scan now and watch a special message from Pastor Joel!

SUNDAY	MONDAY	TUESDAY	WEDNESDAY
1	2	3	4
8	9	10	11
15	16 Presidents' Day (USA)	17	18 Ash Wednesday
22	23	24	25
1	2	3	4

February
MONTHLY VIEW

THURSDAY	FRIDAY	SATURDAY	NOTES
5	6	7	
12 Lincoln's Birthday (USA)	13	14 Valentine's Day	
19	20	21	
26	27	28	
5	6	7	You are deeply loved and eternally cherished by God! — Joel

THIS WEEK'S SCRIPTURE:

. . . God's love has been poured out into our hearts through the Holy Spirit, who has been given to us.

ROMANS 5:5

MY PRAYER THIS WEEK:

TO-DO'S:

- ○ _____
- ○ _____
- ○ _____
- ○ _____
- ○ _____
- ○ _____
- ○ _____
- ○ _____
- ○ _____
- ○ _____

MY *FAITH FOR TODAY* DECLARATION

Because I'm rooted in love, I have nothing to prove and no one to impress. I'm already approved by my Heavenly Father!

February
WEEKLY PLANNING

SUNDAY	MONDAY
1	2

TUESDAY	WEDNESDAY
3	4

THURSDAY	FRIDAY
5	6

SATURDAY	*FAITH FOR TODAY* ACTION
7	Tell someone close to you what you appreciate about them — and be specific.

THIS WEEK I SAW GOD WORKING . . .

I'M CELEBRATING . . . OR LOOKING FORWARD TO . . .

February
WEEKLY REFLECTION

NOTES

THIS WEEK'S SCRIPTURE:

There is no fear in love. But perfect love drives out fear . . .
1 JOHN 4:18

MY PRAYER THIS WEEK:

TO-DO'S:

- ○
- ○
- ○
- ○
- ○
- ○
- ○
- ○
- ○
- ○

MY *FAITH FOR TODAY* DECLARATION

God's love gives me the strength to forgive, courage to speak truth, and peace in every situation.

February
WEEKLY PLANNING

SUNDAY	MONDAY
8	9

TUESDAY	WEDNESDAY
10	11

THURSDAY	FRIDAY
12	13

Lincoln's Birthday (USA)

SATURDAY	FAITH FOR TODAY ACTION
14	Write a note or card to someone who may feel overlooked and remind them they matter.

Valentine's Day

THIS WEEK I SAW GOD WORKING . . .

I'M CELEBRATING . . . OR LOOKING FORWARD TO . . .

February
WEEKLY REFLECTION

NOTES

THIS WEEK'S SCRIPTURE:

And over all these virtues put on love, which binds them all together in perfect unity.

COLOSSIANS 3:14

MY PRAYER THIS WEEK:

TO-DO'S:

-
-
-
-
-
-
-
-
-
-

MY *FAITH FOR TODAY* DECLARATION

I don't have to earn God's love — it's already mine.
I can receive it freely and experience it daily!

February
WEEKLY PLANNING

SUNDAY	MONDAY
15	16
	Presidents' Day (USA)

TUESDAY	WEDNESDAY
17	18
	Ash Wednesday

THURSDAY	FRIDAY
19	20

SATURDAY	FAITH FOR TODAY ACTION
21	Ask God to show you someone who needs encouragement — then send them a text or call and bless them.

THIS WEEK I SAW GOD WORKING . . .

I'M CELEBRATING . . . OR LOOKING FORWARD TO . . .

February
WEEKLY REFLECTION

NOTES

THIS WEEK'S SCRIPTURE:

"As the Father has loved me, so have I loved you. Now remain in my love."

JOHN 15:9

MY PRAYER THIS WEEK:

TO-DO'S:

- ○
- ○
- ○
- ○
- ○
- ○
- ○
- ○
- ○
- ○

MY *FAITH FOR TODAY* DECLARATION

Every step I take is anchored in the love of Christ.
I'm secure, stable, and full of purpose!

February
WEEKLY PLANNING

SUNDAY 22	MONDAY 23
TUESDAY 24	WEDNESDAY 25
THURSDAY 26	FRIDAY 27
SATURDAY 28	**FAITH FOR TODAY ACTION** Serve someone without being asked — a family member, coworker, or neighbor — and do it with joy!

THIS WEEK I SAW GOD WORKING . . .

I'M CELEBRATING . . . OR LOOKING FORWARD TO . . .

February
WEEKLY REFLECTION

NOTES

Every journey has its hills and valleys — seasons where you're full of passion and periods when you feel devoid of purpose. But you are never alone or without help and hope!

This month, let your heart rest in the promise of Isaiah 40:31. When you feel weary, God wants to renew you. When you feel stuck, He longs to lift you. When you feel like you've got nothing left, He reminds you: *"I'm not done with you yet. Wait on Me. Hope in Me. I am your strength!"*

---

*But those who hope in the L*ORD *will renew their strength. They will soar on wings like eagles; they will run and not grow weary, they will walk and not be faint.*
Isaiah 40:31

March
AT-A-GLANCE

THIS MONTH, I'M PUTTING MY FAITH IN GOD FOR:

GOALS & DESIRES THIS MONTH:

TO-DO THIS MONTH

Increase your faith!
Scan now and watch a special message from Pastor Joel!

SUNDAY	MONDAY	TUESDAY	WEDNESDAY
1	2	3	4
8 Daylight Saving Time begins	9	10	11
15	16	17 St. Patrick's Day	18
22	23	24	25
29 Palm Sunday	30	31	1

March
MONTHLY VIEW

THURSDAY	FRIDAY	SATURDAY	NOTES
5	6	7	
12	13	14	
19	20 Spring begins	21	
26	27	28	
2	3	4	The dreams God's given you are treasures worth living for. —Joel

THIS WEEK'S SCRIPTURE:

". . . My grace is sufficient for you, for my power is made perfect in weakness . . ."

2 CORINTHIANS 12:9

MY PRAYER THIS WEEK:

TO-DO'S:

- ○
- ○
- ○
- ○
- ○
- ○
- ○
- ○
- ○
- ○

MY *FAITH FOR TODAY* DECLARATION

I have strength for everything God is calling me to do.
I am equipped and empowered by Him!

March
WEEKLY PLANNING

SUNDAY	MONDAY
1	2

TUESDAY	WEDNESDAY
3	4

THURSDAY	FRIDAY
5	6

SATURDAY	*FAITH FOR TODAY* ACTION
7	Send a message of encouragement to someone who's walking through a hard season — be their reminder of God's grace.

THIS WEEK I SAW GOD WORKING . . .

I'M CELEBRATING . . . OR LOOKING FORWARD TO . . .

March
WEEKLY REFLECTION

NOTES

THIS WEEK'S SCRIPTURE:

God is our refuge and strength, an ever-present help in trouble.
PSALM 46:1

MY PRAYER THIS WEEK: TO-DO'S:

○ _____
○ _____
○ _____
○ _____
○ _____
○ _____
○ _____
○ _____
○ _____
○ _____

MY *FAITH FOR TODAY* DECLARATION

Even when the path feels long, I won't give up —
God's strength is renewing me each day.

March
WEEKLY PLANNING

SUNDAY
8

Daylight Saving Time begins

MONDAY
9

TUESDAY
10

WEDNESDAY
11

THURSDAY
12

FRIDAY
13

SATURDAY
14

FAITH FOR TODAY ACTION
Offer to help carry someone's load — babysit, cook a meal, run an errand, or mow a lawn.

THIS WEEK I SAW GOD WORKING . . .

I'M CELEBRATING . . . OR LOOKING FORWARD TO . . .

March
WEEKLY REFLECTION

NOTES

THIS WEEK'S SCRIPTURE:

I can do all this through him who gives me strength.
PHILIPPIANS 4:13

MY PRAYER THIS WEEK: **TO-DO'S:**

- ○
- ○
- ○
- ○
- ○
- ○
- ○
- ○
- ○
- ○

MY *FAITH FOR TODAY* DECLARATION

I am not running on empty — I'm sustained by grace,
and God's supply never runs out.

March
WEEKLY PLANNING

SUNDAY	MONDAY
15	16

TUESDAY	WEDNESDAY
17	18

St. Patrick's Day

THURSDAY	FRIDAY
19	20

Spring begins

SATURDAY	*FAITH FOR TODAY* ACTION
21	Pray out loud over a friend or loved one this week. Ask God to strengthen and uplift them.

THIS WEEK I SAW GOD WORKING . . .

I'M CELEBRATING . . . OR LOOKING FORWARD TO . . .

March

WEEKLY REFLECTION

NOTES

THIS WEEK'S SCRIPTURE:

"The Lord himself goes before you and will be with you; he will never leave you nor forsake you . . ."

DEUTERONOMY 31:8

MY PRAYER THIS WEEK: **TO-DO'S:**

- ○
- ○
- ○
- ○
- ○
- ○
- ○
- ○
- ○
- ○

MY *FAITH FOR TODAY* DECLARATION

When I feel weak, I lean into God's power.
His strength is made perfect in me.

March
WEEKLY PLANNING

SUNDAY 22	**MONDAY** 23
TUESDAY 24	**WEDNESDAY** 25
THURSDAY 26	**FRIDAY** 27
SATURDAY 28	**FAITH FOR TODAY ACTION** Start a "strength thread" with a group of friends — share wins, verses, and prayers to build each other up.

THIS WEEK I SAW GOD WORKING...

I'M CELEBRATING... OR LOOKING FORWARD TO...

March
WEEKLY REFLECTION

NOTES

Jesus is risen! And because He rose, you can live with hope, purpose, and the unshakable confidence that nothing is too hard for God.

As you celebrate Easter this month, recognize that it's more than a holiday; it's a reminder of your reality. What was dead can come back to life. What looks hopeless can turn around. What feels buried — your dream, your purpose, even your peace — can be resurrected.

The same Spirit that raised Christ from the dead lives in you. That means you carry resurrection power — the power to overcome sin, rise out of discouragement, break free from fear, and walk into the fullness of your calling. Throw away the graveclothes. Shake off the past. Your Savior conquered the grave — and He's still bringing dead things to life!

And if the Spirit of him who raised Jesus from the dead is living in you, he who raised Christ from the dead will also give life to your mortal bodies because of his Spirit who lives in you.
Romans 8:11

April
AT-A-GLANCE

THIS MONTH, I'M PUTTING MY FAITH IN GOD FOR:

_____

_____

_____

_____

_____

_____

GOALS & DESIRES THIS MONTH:

TO-DO THIS MONTH

- ○ _____
- ○ _____
- ○ _____
- ○ _____
- ○ _____
- ○ _____
- ○ _____

Increase your faith!
Scan now and watch a special message from Pastor Joel!

SUNDAY	MONDAY	TUESDAY	WEDNESDAY
29	30	31	1
5 Easter / Resurrection Sunday	6	7	8
12	13	14	15
19	20	21	22
26	27	28	29

April
MONTHLY VIEW

THURSDAY	FRIDAY	SATURDAY
2	3 Good Friday	4
9	10	11
16	17	18
23	24	25
30	1	2

NOTES

You have hope for the future. You're alive in Christ!

— Joel

THIS WEEK'S SCRIPTURE:

*We were therefore buried with him through baptism into death . . .
[that] we too may live a new life.*

ROMANS 6:4

MY PRAYER THIS WEEK:　　　　　　　　　**TO-DO'S:**

-
-
-
-
-
-
-
-
-
-

MY *FAITH FOR TODAY* DECLARATION

The same Spirit and power that raised Jesus from the dead now lives in me — giving me purpose and strength!

April
WEEKLY PLANNING

SUNDAY	MONDAY
29	30
Palm Sunday	

TUESDAY	WEDNESDAY
31	1

THURSDAY	FRIDAY
2	3
	Good Friday

SATURDAY	FAITH FOR TODAY ACTION
4	Invite someone to church this Easter — someone who needs to hear that new life is possible!

THIS WEEK I SAW GOD WORKING . . .

I'M CELEBRATING . . . OR LOOKING FORWARD TO . . .

April
WEEKLY REFLECTION

NOTES

THIS WEEK'S SCRIPTURE:

I want to know Christ — yes, to know the power of his resurrection . . .

PHILIPPIANS 3:10

MY PRAYER THIS WEEK: TO-DO'S:

-
-
-
-
-
-
-
-
-
-

MY *FAITH FOR TODAY* DECLARATION

What looked dead is being revived. Even now, God is breathing new life into my future!

April
WEEKLY PLANNING

SUNDAY	MONDAY
5	6
Easter / Resurrection Sunday	

TUESDAY	WEDNESDAY
7	8

THURSDAY	FRIDAY
9	10

SATURDAY	*FAITH FOR TODAY* ACTION
11	Send a message to someone who's struggling: "I'm praying for resurrection life to fill your heart this week, in Jesus' name."

THIS WEEK I SAW GOD WORKING . . .

I'M CELEBRATING . . . OR LOOKING FORWARD TO . . .

April
WEEKLY REFLECTION

NOTES

THIS WEEK'S SCRIPTURE:

Praise be to the God and Father of our Lord Jesus Christ! In his great mercy he has given us new birth into a living hope through the resurrection of Jesus Christ from the dead.

1 PETER 1:3

MY PRAYER THIS WEEK:

TO-DO'S:

- ○ _____
- ○ _____
- ○ _____
- ○ _____
- ○ _____
- ○ _____
- ○ _____
- ○ _____
- ○ _____
- ○ _____

MY *FAITH FOR TODAY* DECLARATION

I am not a victim of my past — I am a victor through the power of the resurrection!

April
WEEKLY PLANNING

SUNDAY 12	MONDAY 13
TUESDAY 14	WEDNESDAY 15
THURSDAY 16	FRIDAY 17
SATURDAY 18	**FAITH FOR TODAY ACTION** Give a small gift or handwritten card to someone who may feel forgotten.

THIS WEEK I SAW GOD WORKING . . .

I'M CELEBRATING . . . OR LOOKING FORWARD TO . . .

April
WEEKLY REFLECTION

NOTES

THIS WEEK'S SCRIPTURE:

". . . I am the resurrection and the life. The one who believes in me will live, even though they die."

JOHN 11:25

MY PRAYER THIS WEEK:　　　　　　　**TO-DO'S:**

-
-
-
-
-
-
-
-
-
-

MY *FAITH FOR TODAY* DECLARATION

Because Jesus rose, I rise — overcoming fear, conquering discouragement, and experiencing victory instead of defeat.

April
WEEKLY PLANNING

SUNDAY 19	MONDAY 20
TUESDAY 21	WEDNESDAY 22
THURSDAY 23	FRIDAY 24
SATURDAY 25	**FAITH FOR TODAY ACTION**
	Share a personal testimony with someone of how God brought something dead back to life — it may stir up their faith!

THIS WEEK I SAW GOD WORKING . . .

I'M CELEBRATING . . . OR LOOKING FORWARD TO . . .

April
WEEKLY REFLECTION

NOTES

THIS WEEK'S SCRIPTURE:

By his power God raised the Lord from the dead, and he will raise us also.

1 CORINTHIANS 6:14

MY PRAYER THIS WEEK:					TO-DO'S:

-
-
-
-
-
-
-
-
-
-

MY *FAITH FOR TODAY* DECLARATION

God isn't finished with me — this is my season for renewal and resurrection!

April
WEEKLY PLANNING

SUNDAY	MONDAY
26	27

TUESDAY	WEDNESDAY
28	29

THURSDAY	FRIDAY
30	1

SATURDAY	*FAITH FOR TODAY* ACTION
2	Surprise someone with "new life" generosity — buy them groceries, pay their bill, or bless them anonymously.

THIS WEEK I SAW GOD WORKING . . .

I'M CELEBRATING . . . OR LOOKING FORWARD TO . . .

April
WEEKLY REFLECTION

NOTES

When God's favor is on your life, you can bloom right where you are.

According to Jeremiah 17:7–8, you are like a tree planted by streams of water. That means your strength doesn't come from what's around you — it comes from who you belong to. Even in dry seasons, even when others are shrinking back, you can thrive. Why? Because your source isn't circumstances — it's God!

This month, let go of the idea you must "arrive" somewhere before you can grow. Look for how God wants to favor you where you are because there are undoubtedly blessings to discover in your "now." There is purpose in your present. And the favor of God isn't limited by the location you're in or the conditions surrounding you. In a moment, He can cause you to flourish. Stay expectant. And get ready — you're about to see favor flow in unexpected ways!

"But blessed is the one who trusts in the LORD, whose confidence is in him. They will be like a tree planted by the water. . . . Its leaves are always green. It has no worries in a year of drought and never fails to bear fruit."
Jeremiah 17:7–8

May
AT-A-GLANCE

THIS MONTH, I'M PUTTING MY FAITH IN GOD FOR:

GOALS & DESIRES THIS MONTH:

TO-DO THIS MONTH

Increase your faith!
Scan now and watch a special message from Pastor Joel!

SUNDAY	MONDAY	TUESDAY	WEDNESDAY
26	27	28	29
3	4	5	6
10 Mother's Day	11	12	13
17	18 Victoria Day (CAN)	19	20
24 / 31	25 Memorial Day (USA)	26	27

May
MONTHLY VIEW

THURSDAY	FRIDAY	SATURDAY	NOTES
30	1	2	
7 National Day of Prayer	8	9	
14	15	16	
21	22	23	
28	29	30	Trust God. With Him, the impossible becomes possible! — Joel

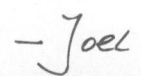

THIS WEEK'S SCRIPTURE:

That person is like a tree planted by streams of water . . . whatever they do prospers.

PSALM 1:3

MY PRAYER THIS WEEK: **TO-DO'S:**

MY *FAITH FOR TODAY* DECLARATION

I am planted in God's promises, and I'm able to flourish in every season!

May
WEEKLY PLANNING

SUNDAY 3	**MONDAY** 4
TUESDAY 5	**WEDNESDAY** 6
THURSDAY 7 National Day of Prayer	**FRIDAY** 8
SATURDAY 9	**FAITH FOR TODAY ACTION** Encourage someone who's in a "waiting place" — remind them God is working even now.

THIS WEEK I SAW GOD WORKING . . .

I'M CELEBRATING . . . OR LOOKING FORWARD TO . . .

May
WEEKLY REFLECTION

NOTES

THIS WEEK'S SCRIPTURE:

"The LORD will guide you always. . . . You will be like a well-watered garden . . ."

ISAIAH 58:11

MY PRAYER THIS WEEK:

TO-DO'S:

○ _____
○ _____
○ _____
○ _____
○ _____
○ _____
○ _____
○ _____
○ _____
○ _____

MY *FAITH FOR TODAY* DECLARATION

I may not be where I want to be, but I'm favored right where I am.

May
WEEKLY PLANNING

SUNDAY
10

Mother's Day

MONDAY
11

TUESDAY
12

WEDNESDAY
13

THURSDAY
14

FRIDAY
15

SATURDAY
16

FAITH FOR TODAY ACTION
Bless someone unexpectedly at your workplace or in your neighborhood.

THIS WEEK I SAW GOD WORKING . . .

I'M CELEBRATING . . . OR LOOKING FORWARD TO . . .

May
WEEKLY REFLECTION

NOTES

THIS WEEK'S SCRIPTURE:

The Lord was with [Joseph]; he showed him kindness and granted him favor . . .

GENESIS 39:21

MY PRAYER THIS WEEK:

TO-DO'S:

- ○
- ○
- ○
- ○
- ○
- ○
- ○
- ○
- ○
- ○

MY *FAITH FOR TODAY* DECLARATION

God's favor surrounds me today like a shield — opening doors and making a way.

May
WEEKLY PLANNING

SUNDAY 17	MONDAY 18
	Victoria Day (CAN)

TUESDAY 19	WEDNESDAY 20

THURSDAY 21	FRIDAY 22

SATURDAY 23	*FAITH FOR TODAY* ACTION
	Send a thank-you message to someone who's helped you grow in your faith this year.

THIS WEEK I SAW GOD WORKING . . .

I'M CELEBRATING . . . OR LOOKING FORWARD TO . . .

May
WEEKLY REFLECTION

NOTES

THIS WEEK'S SCRIPTURE:

May the favor of the Lord our God rest on us; establish the work of our hands . . .

PSALM 90:17

MY PRAYER THIS WEEK:

TO-DO'S:

- ○
- ○
- ○
- ○
- ○
- ○
- ○
- ○
- ○
- ○

MY *FAITH FOR TODAY* DECLARATION

Where I am isn't where I'll stay — God is preparing me for more!

May
WEEKLY PLANNING

SUNDAY	MONDAY
24	25
	Memorial Day (USA)

TUESDAY	WEDNESDAY
26	27

THURSDAY	FRIDAY
28	29

SATURDAY	*FAITH FOR TODAY* ACTION
30	Do something creative to bring life to your space (home, office, church, etc.).

THIS WEEK I SAW GOD WORKING . . .

I'M CELEBRATING . . . OR LOOKING FORWARD TO . . .

May
WEEKLY REFLECTION

NOTES

The spirit God gave you isn't one of fear, timidity, or hesitation. It's one of power, love, and a sound mind!

Even when you feel uncertain, you can know that God is in control. Even if you don't have all the answers, you can boldly step forward. Even when fear raises its voice, you can speak out God's promises. In the strength and power of the Holy Spirit, you can put your faith in the One who never fails, positioning yourself for favor, breakthrough, and victory!

For the Spirit God gave us does not make us timid, but gives us power, love and self-discipline.
2 Timothy 1:7

June
AT-A-GLANCE

THIS MONTH, I'M PUTTING MY FAITH IN GOD FOR:

_____

_____

_____

_____

_____

GOALS & DESIRES THIS MONTH:

TO-DO THIS MONTH

- _____
- _____
- _____
- _____
- _____
- _____
- _____

Increase your faith!
Scan now and watch a special message from Pastor Joel!

SUNDAY	MONDAY	TUESDAY	WEDNESDAY
31	1	2	3
7	8	9	10
14	15	16	17
21	22	23	24
Father's Day / Summer begins			
28	29	30	1

June
MONTHLY VIEW

THURSDAY	FRIDAY	SATURDAY
4	5	6
11	12	13
18	19	20
	Juneteenth (USA)	
25	26	27
2	3	4

NOTES

Your Heavenly Father is always working things for your good.

— Joel

THIS WEEK'S SCRIPTURE:

*"So do not fear, for I am with you. . . .
I will strengthen you and help you . . ."*

ISAIAH 41:10

MY PRAYER THIS WEEK: **TO-DO'S:**

○ _____

○ _____

○ _____

○ _____

○ _____

○ _____

○ _____

○ _____

○ _____

○ _____

MY *FAITH FOR TODAY* DECLARATION

Fear has no hold on me — God has filled me with courage, confidence, and clarity!

June
WEEKLY PLANNING

SUNDAY	MONDAY
31	1

TUESDAY	WEDNESDAY
2	3

THURSDAY	FRIDAY
4	5

SATURDAY	*FAITH FOR TODAY* ACTION
6	Call or text someone who's walking through a difficult time and ask if you can pray for them.

THIS WEEK I SAW GOD WORKING . . .

I'M CELEBRATING . . . OR LOOKING FORWARD TO . . .

June
WEEKLY REFLECTION

NOTES

THIS WEEK'S SCRIPTURE:

When I am afraid, I put my trust in you.
PSALM 56:3

MY PRAYER THIS WEEK:

TO-DO'S:

-
-
-
-
-
-
-
-
-
-

MY *FAITH FOR TODAY* DECLARATION

I walk by faith, not by feelings. Even when I'm unsure,
I trust that God is with me.

June
WEEKLY PLANNING

SUNDAY 7	MONDAY 8
TUESDAY 9	WEDNESDAY 10
THURSDAY 11	FRIDAY 12
SATURDAY 13	**FAITH FOR TODAY ACTION** Share your testimony of overcoming fear — it might be exactly what someone else needs to hear.

THIS WEEK I SAW GOD WORKING . . .

I'M CELEBRATING . . . OR LOOKING FORWARD TO . . .

June

WEEKLY REFLECTION

NOTES

THIS WEEK'S SCRIPTURE:

*"Be strong and courageous. . . .
The LORD your God goes with you . . ."*

DEUTERONOMY 31:6

MY PRAYER THIS WEEK:

TO-DO'S:

-
-
-
-
-
-
-
-
-
-

MY *FAITH FOR TODAY* DECLARATION

I am strong, bold, and equipped for everything
God is calling me to do.

June
WEEKLY PLANNING

SUNDAY	MONDAY
14	15

TUESDAY	WEDNESDAY
16	17

THURSDAY	FRIDAY
18	19
	Juneteenth

SATURDAY	**FAITH FOR TODAY ACTION**
20	Invite someone to church or a small group — fear isolates, but faith gathers.

THIS WEEK I SAW GOD WORKING . . .

I'M CELEBRATING . . . OR LOOKING FORWARD TO . . .

June
WEEKLY REFLECTION

NOTES

THIS WEEK'S SCRIPTURE:

"Peace I leave with you; my peace I give you. . . . Do not let your hearts be troubled and do not be afraid."

JOHN 14:27

MY PRAYER THIS WEEK:　　　　　　　　　**TO-DO'S:**

- ○ _____
- ○ _____
- ○ _____
- ○ _____
- ○ _____
- ○ _____
- ○ _____
- ○ _____
- ○ _____
- ○ _____

MY *FAITH FOR TODAY* DECLARATION

No matter what I face, I choose faith over fear, peace over panic, and trust over anxiety.

june
WEEKLY PLANNING

SUNDAY	MONDAY
21	22

Father's Day / Summer begins

TUESDAY	WEDNESDAY
23	24

THURSDAY	FRIDAY
25	26

SATURDAY	FAITH FOR TODAY ACTION
27	Bless someone in a bold way this week — pay for their meal, write them a word of encouragement, or show up unexpectedly to support them.

THIS WEEK I SAW GOD WORKING...

I'M CELEBRATING... OR LOOKING FORWARD TO...

June
WEEKLY REFLECTION

NOTES

Freedom isn't just about what you've been set free from — it's about what you've been set free for.

You've been released *from* fear, guilt, and limitation. But you've also been released into boldness, purpose, and possibility. And God wants to breathe life back *into* your dreams — the ones that seem too big, too far, and too unlikely. Because those are the kinds of dreams He specializes in!

You weren't created to live a small, restricted life. You were created to dream big dreams with a big God. And there is freedom in Christ to believe again. To imagine new things. To step out in faith. To say, "God, I don't know how You'll do it, but I believe You can." So shake off the limitations. Let go of "what if" fears. Make space in your heart to dream again — because with God, there's no limit to what's possible!

Now to him who is able to do immeasurably more than all we ask or imagine, according to his power that is at work within us.
Ephesians 3:20

July
AT-A-GLANCE

THIS MONTH, I'M PUTTING MY FAITH IN GOD FOR:

GOALS & DESIRES THIS MONTH:

TO-DO THIS MONTH

Increase your faith!
Scan now and watch a special message from Pastor Joel!

SUNDAY	MONDAY	TUESDAY	WEDNESDAY
28	29	30	1 Canada Day (CAN)
5	6	7	8
12	13	14	15
19	20	21	22
26	27	28	29

July
MONTHLY VIEW

THURSDAY	FRIDAY	SATURDAY
2	3	4 Independence Day
9	10	11
16	17	18
23	24	25
30	31	1

NOTES

God is with you and faithful to His promises!

— Joel

THIS WEEK'S SCRIPTURE:

*"For I know the plans I have for you," declares the L*ORD*,
"plans to . . . give you hope and a future."*

JEREMIAH 29:11

MY PRAYER THIS WEEK: **TO-DO'S:**

- ○
- ○
- ○
- ○
- ○
- ○
- ○
- ○
- ○
- ○

MY *FAITH FOR TODAY* DECLARATION

I am free in Christ — and free to dream bigger than ever before.

July
WEEKLY PLANNING

SUNDAY	MONDAY
28	29

TUESDAY	WEDNESDAY
30	1
	Canada Day (CAN)

THURSDAY	FRIDAY
2	3

SATURDAY	**FAITH FOR TODAY ACTION**
4	Ask someone close to you, "What's a dream God put in your heart?" — and then cheer them on!

Independence Day

THIS WEEK I SAW GOD WORKING . . .

I'M CELEBRATING . . . OR LOOKING FORWARD TO . . .

July
WEEKLY REFLECTION

NOTES

THIS WEEK'S SCRIPTURE:

*Commit to the Lord whatever you do,
and he will establish your plans.*

PROVERBS 16:3

MY PRAYER THIS WEEK: **TO-DO'S:**

- ○
- ○
- ○
- ○
- ○
- ○
- ○
- ○
- ○
- ○

MY *FAITH FOR TODAY* DECLARATION

God's power is working in me, and I believe He's doing more than I can imagine!

# July
WEEKLY PLANNING

SUNDAY	MONDAY
5	6

TUESDAY	WEDNESDAY
7	8

THURSDAY	FRIDAY
9	10

SATURDAY	*FAITH FOR TODAY* ACTION
11	Write an encouraging message to someone who's starting something new — help them believe they can do it.

THIS WEEK I SAW GOD WORKING . . .

I'M CELEBRATING . . . OR LOOKING FORWARD TO . . .

July
WEEKLY REFLECTION

NOTES

THIS WEEK'S SCRIPTURE:

*Take delight in the L*ORD*, and he will give you the desires of your heart.*

PSALM 37:4

MY PRAYER THIS WEEK:

TO-DO'S:

- ○ _____
- ○ _____
- ○ _____
- ○ _____
- ○ _____
- ○ _____
- ○ _____
- ○ _____
- ○ _____
- ○ _____

MY *FAITH FOR TODAY* DECLARATION

In faith, I release fear, failure, and doubt. In Jesus' name,
I embrace possibility, purpose, and bold vision!

July
WEEKLY PLANNING

SUNDAY 12	MONDAY 13
TUESDAY 14	WEDNESDAY 15
THURSDAY 16	FRIDAY 17
SATURDAY 18	**FAITH FOR TODAY ACTION** Support someone else's dream this month — give, show up, volunteer, or connect them with an encouraging resource.

THIS WEEK I SAW GOD WORKING . . .

I'M CELEBRATING . . . OR LOOKING FORWARD TO . . .

July
WEEKLY REFLECTION

NOTES

THIS WEEK'S SCRIPTURE:

". . . Write down the revelation and make it plain. . . . Though it linger, wait for it; it will certainly come . . ."

HABAKKUK 2:2–3

MY PRAYER THIS WEEK:

TO-DO'S:

-
-
-
-
-
-
-
-
-
-

MY *FAITH FOR TODAY* DECLARATION

My past can't limit me. God is writing a new future for me, filled with hope and greatness!

July
WEEKLY PLANNING

SUNDAY	MONDAY
19	20

TUESDAY	WEDNESDAY
21	22

THURSDAY	FRIDAY
23	24

SATURDAY	*FAITH FOR TODAY* ACTION
25	Share your own testimony of how God fulfilled a dream in your life — it may inspire someone else to dream again.

THIS WEEK I SAW GOD WORKING . . .

I'M CELEBRATING . . . OR LOOKING FORWARD TO . . .

July
WEEKLY REFLECTION

NOTES

THIS WEEK'S SCRIPTURE:

*The Spirit you received does not make you slaves,
so that you live in fear again . . .*

ROMANS 8:15

MY PRAYER THIS WEEK:		TO-DO'S:

○ _____
○ _____
○ _____
○ _____
○ _____
○ _____
○ _____
○ _____
○ _____
○ _____

MY *FAITH FOR TODAY* DECLARATION

I won't be limited by fear — I am stepping into
all God has prepared for me!

July
WEEKLY PLANNING

SUNDAY	MONDAY
26	27

TUESDAY	WEDNESDAY
28	29

THURSDAY	FRIDAY
30	31

SATURDAY	*FAITH FOR TODAY* ACTION
1	Speak words of life over someone who's doubting themselves. Remind them what God says about who they are.

THIS WEEK I SAW GOD WORKING...

I'M CELEBRATING... OR LOOKING FORWARD TO...

July
WEEKLY REFLECTION

NOTES

What may feel broken, buried, or beyond repair isn't the end of your story. God can restore, renew, and rewrite your future with grace and power!

Whether it's your confidence, peace, purpose, finances, or relationships — you're not starting over from scratch. You're beginning again with God's help, God's favor, and God's plan. What you've walked through has prepared you for what He's about to build through you. The rubble isn't the end — it's the raw material for a testimony of renewal.

Pick up your faith again. Dust off your hope. The One on the throne is declaring over you: *"I am making all things new!"*

He who was seated on the throne said,
"I am making everything new!" . . .
Revelation 21:5

August
AT-A-GLANCE

THIS MONTH, I'M PUTTING MY FAITH IN GOD FOR:

GOALS & DESIRES THIS MONTH:

TO-DO THIS MONTH

Increase your faith!
Scan now and watch a special message from Pastor Joel!

SUNDAY	MONDAY	TUESDAY	WEDNESDAY
26	27	28	29
2	3 Civic Day (CAN)	4	5
9	10	11	12
16	17	18	19
23 30	24 31	25	26

August
MONTHLY VIEW

THURSDAY	FRIDAY	SATURDAY
30	31	1
6	7	8
13	14	15
20	21	22
27	28	29

NOTES

God is with you and faithful to His promises!

— Joel

THIS WEEK'S SCRIPTURE:

They will rebuild the ancient ruins and restore the places long devastated . . .

ISAIAH 61:4

MY PRAYER THIS WEEK: **TO-DO'S:**

○ _____
○ _____
○ _____
○ _____
○ _____
○ _____
○ _____
○ _____
○ _____
○ _____

MY *FAITH FOR TODAY* DECLARATION

I will not be defined by my ruins. God is laying a foundation for something greater.

August
WEEKLY PLANNING

SUNDAY	MONDAY
2	3 Civic Day (CAN)

TUESDAY	WEDNESDAY
4	5

THURSDAY	FRIDAY
6	7

SATURDAY	*FAITH FOR TODAY* ACTION
8	Help someone rebuild — offer your time, skills, or encouragement to someone starting over.

THIS WEEK I SAW GOD WORKING . . .

I'M CELEBRATING . . . OR LOOKING FORWARD TO . . .

August
WEEKLY REFLECTION

NOTES

THIS WEEK'S SCRIPTURE:

They were all trying to frighten us. . . . But I prayed, "Now strengthen my hands."

NEHEMIAH 6:9

MY PRAYER THIS WEEK: **TO-DO'S:**

- ○
- ○
- ○
- ○
- ○
- ○
- ○
- ○
- ○
- ○

MY *FAITH FOR TODAY* DECLARATION

What was broken will be restored. What was delayed will be fulfilled. In Jesus' name!

August
WEEKLY PLANNING

SUNDAY 9	MONDAY 10

TUESDAY 11	WEDNESDAY 12

THURSDAY 13	FRIDAY 14

SATURDAY 15	*FAITH FOR TODAY* ACTION
	Share a testimony of how God rebuilt something in your life — it may give someone else hope to keep going.

THIS WEEK I SAW GOD WORKING . . .

I'M CELEBRATING . . . OR LOOKING FORWARD TO . . .

August
WEEKLY REFLECTION

NOTES

THIS WEEK'S SCRIPTURE:

"I will repay you for the years the locusts have eaten . . ."
JOEL 2:25

MY PRAYER THIS WEEK:

TO-DO'S:

- ○
- ○
- ○
- ○
- ○
- ○
- ○
- ○
- ○
- ○

MY *FAITH FOR TODAY* DECLARATION

Every setback is a setup for God to show His faithfulness in my life.

August
WEEKLY PLANNING

SUNDAY
16

MONDAY
17

TUESDAY
18

WEDNESDAY
19

THURSDAY
20

FRIDAY
21

SATURDAY
22

FAITH FOR TODAY ACTION
Encourage a friend who's facing disappointment with these words: "You're not starting over — God is building something better."

THIS WEEK I SAW GOD WORKING . . .

I'M CELEBRATING . . . OR LOOKING FORWARD TO . . .

August
WEEKLY REFLECTION

NOTES

THIS WEEK'S SCRIPTURE:

Those who sow with tears will reap with songs of joy.
PSALM 126:5

MY PRAYER THIS WEEK: **TO-DO'S:**

- ○ _____
- ○ _____
- ○ _____
- ○ _____
- ○ _____
- ○ _____
- ○ _____
- ○ _____
- ○ _____
- ○ _____

MY *FAITH FOR TODAY* DECLARATION
I have the strength to rise, the courage to rebuild, and the favor of God to finish strong.

August
WEEKLY PLANNING

SUNDAY	MONDAY
23	24

TUESDAY	WEDNESDAY
25	26

THURSDAY	FRIDAY
27	28

SATURDAY	FAITH FOR TODAY ACTION
29	Donate or serve in a local organization helping people rebuild their lives — be part of someone else's comeback story.

THIS WEEK I SAW GOD WORKING . . .

I'M CELEBRATING . . . OR LOOKING FORWARD TO . . .

August
WEEKLY REFLECTION

NOTES

Your thoughts can affect everything — determining your focus, fueling your faith, and influencing how you experience every part of your day.

Do you want a more hopeful perspective? Desiring peace? Praying for an outpouring of faith and favor? This month, renew your mind with God's truth and possibility. Replace fearful and anxious thinking with thoughts that are rooted in faith and filled with hope. As you do this, you're on your way to God's best for you!

Finally, brothers and sisters, whatever is true, whatever is noble, whatever is right, whatever is pure, whatever is lovely, whatever is admirable — if anything is excellent or praiseworthy — think about such things.
Philippians 4:8

September
AT-A-GLANCE

THIS MONTH, I'M PUTTING MY FAITH IN GOD FOR:

_____
_____
_____
_____
_____
_____

GOALS & DESIRES THIS MONTH:

TO-DO THIS MONTH

- ◯ _____
- ◯ _____
- ◯ _____
- ◯ _____
- ◯ _____
- ◯ _____
- ◯ _____

Increase your faith!
Scan now and watch a special message from Pastor Joel!

SUNDAY	MONDAY	TUESDAY	WEDNESDAY
30	31	1	2
6	7 Labor Day	8	9
13	14	15	16
20	21	22 Fall begins	23
27	28	29	30

September
MONTHLY VIEW

THURSDAY	FRIDAY	SATURDAY
3	4	5
10	11	12
17	18	19
24	25	26
1	2	3

NOTES

Your faith activates God's power in and around you.

—Joel

THIS WEEK'S SCRIPTURE:

Do not conform to the pattern of this world, but be transformed by the renewing of your mind . . .

ROMANS 12:2

MY PRAYER THIS WEEK:

TO-DO'S:

○ _____
○ _____
○ _____
○ _____
○ _____
○ _____
○ _____
○ _____
○ _____
○ _____

MY *FAITH FOR TODAY* DECLARATION

I reject fear and worry and fix my mind on God's promises and peace.

September
WEEKLY PLANNING

SUNDAY	MONDAY
30	31

TUESDAY	WEDNESDAY
1	2

THURSDAY	FRIDAY
3	4

SATURDAY	FAITH FOR TODAY ACTION
5	Encourage someone who's overwhelmed — speak peace, truth, and hope over them.

THIS WEEK I SAW GOD WORKING . . .

I'M CELEBRATING . . . OR LOOKING FORWARD TO . . .

September
WEEKLY REFLECTION

NOTES

THIS WEEK'S SCRIPTURE:

. . . We take captive every thought to make it obedient to Christ.
2 CORINTHIANS 10:5

MY PRAYER THIS WEEK:

TO-DO'S:

-
-
-
-
-
-
-
-
-
-

MY *FAITH FOR TODAY* DECLARATION

I'm not stuck in negative thinking — I have the mind of Christ!

September
WEEKLY PLANNING

SUNDAY
6

MONDAY
7

Labor Day

TUESDAY
8

WEDNESDAY
9

THURSDAY
10

FRIDAY
11

SATURDAY
12

FAITH FOR TODAY ACTION
Ask someone who's walked through what you're facing for advice and encouragement.

THIS WEEK I SAW GOD WORKING . . .

I'M CELEBRATING . . . OR LOOKING FORWARD TO . . .

September
WEEKLY REFLECTION

NOTES

THIS WEEK'S SCRIPTURE:

Set your minds on things above, not on earthly things.
COLOSSIANS 3:2

MY PRAYER THIS WEEK:

TO-DO'S:

- ○
- ○
- ○
- ○
- ○
- ○
- ○
- ○
- ○
- ○

MY *FAITH FOR TODAY* DECLARATION

God is renewing my mind, reshaping my perspective, and restoring my hope.

September
WEEKLY PLANNING

SUNDAY	MONDAY
13	14

TUESDAY	WEDNESDAY
15	16

THURSDAY	FRIDAY
17	18

SATURDAY	*FAITH FOR TODAY* ACTION
19	Lead a younger person or mentee by example. Show them what walking with peace and wisdom looks like.

THIS WEEK I SAW GOD WORKING . . .

I'M CELEBRATING . . . OR LOOKING FORWARD TO . . .

September
WEEKLY REFLECTION

NOTES

THIS WEEK'S SCRIPTURE:

You will keep in perfect peace those whose minds are steadfast, because they trust in you.

ISAIAH 26:3

MY PRAYER THIS WEEK:

TO-DO'S:

- ○
- ○
- ○
- ○
- ○
- ○
- ○
- ○
- ○
- ○

MY *FAITH FOR TODAY* DECLARATION

Every thought I dwell on will move me closer to God's best for my life.

September
WEEKLY PLANNING

SUNDAY 20	MONDAY 21

TUESDAY 22	WEDNESDAY 23
Fall begins	

THURSDAY 24	FRIDAY 25

SATURDAY 26	*FAITH FOR TODAY* ACTION
	Speak life over someone who feels uncertain. Remind them that God will give them wisdom as they seek Him.

THIS WEEK I SAW GOD WORKING . . .

I'M CELEBRATING . . . OR LOOKING FORWARD TO . . .

September
WEEKLY REFLECTION

NOTES

THIS WEEK'S SCRIPTURE:

*Let us hold unswervingly to the hope we profess,
for he who promised is faithful.*

HEBREWS 10:23

MY PRAYER THIS WEEK: TO-DO'S:

○ _____

○ _____

○ _____

○ _____

○ _____

○ _____

○ _____

○ _____

○ _____

○ _____

MY *FAITH FOR TODAY* DECLARATION

This week I receive the mind of Christ and set my focus on His truth and hope for me. Fear and stress are not my future — victory is!

September
WEEKLY PLANNING

SUNDAY	MONDAY
27	28

TUESDAY	WEDNESDAY
29	30

THURSDAY	FRIDAY
1	2

SATURDAY	FAITH FOR TODAY ACTION
3	Is there anyone in your life you struggle to love or connect with? This week, focus on thinking positively about them. And pray for them when they come to mind.

THIS WEEK I SAW GOD WORKING . . .

I'M CELEBRATING . . . OR LOOKING FORWARD TO . . .

September
WEEKLY REFLECTION

NOTES

Through Jesus, the battle has already been won, and the victory is yours! Lack, addiction, anxiety, generational cycles — nothing can hold you back when God has already declared you are free.

You're closer to your breakthrough than you think. Stop asking, "Can I do this?" and start declaring, "God is already doing this in me." In Jesus' name, believe and declare that chains are breaking, doors are opening, and what seemed stuck is about to move. Your breakthrough isn't a "maybe." It's a promise God will fulfill!

But thanks be to God! He gives us the victory through our Lord Jesus Christ.
1 Corinthians 15:57

October
AT-A-GLANCE

THIS MONTH, I'M PUTTING MY FAITH IN GOD FOR:

GOALS & DESIRES THIS MONTH:

TO-DO THIS MONTH

Increase your faith!
Scan now and watch a special message from Pastor Joel!

SUNDAY	MONDAY	TUESDAY	WEDNESDAY
27	28	29	30
4	5	6	7
11	12 Columbus Day (USA) / Thanksgiving Day (CAN)	13	14
18	19	20	21
25	26	27	28

October
MONTHLY VIEW

THURSDAY	FRIDAY	SATURDAY
1	2	3
8	9	10
15	16	17
22	23	24
29	30	31 Halloween

NOTES

You cannot expect victory and plan for defeat.

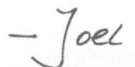

— Joel

THIS WEEK'S SCRIPTURE:

"The One who breaks open the way will go up before them . . ."
MICAH 2:13

MY PRAYER THIS WEEK: **TO-DO'S:**

○ _____
○ _____
○ _____
○ _____
○ _____
○ _____
○ _____
○ _____
○ _____
○ _____

MY *FAITH FOR TODAY* DECLARATION

Every wall in my life is coming down — God is breaking through where I couldn't.

October
WEEKLY PLANNING

SUNDAY	MONDAY
4	5

TUESDAY	WEDNESDAY
6	7

THURSDAY	FRIDAY
8	9

SATURDAY	*FAITH FOR TODAY* ACTION
10	Encourage someone who's still in the fight — remind them that God finishes what He starts.

THIS WEEK I SAW GOD WORKING . . .

I'M CELEBRATING . . . OR LOOKING FORWARD TO . . .

October
WEEKLY REFLECTION

NOTES

THIS WEEK'S SCRIPTURE:

With your help I can advance against a troop; with my God I can scale a wall.

PSALM 18:29

MY PRAYER THIS WEEK:

TO-DO'S:

- ○ _____
- ○ _____
- ○ _____
- ○ _____
- ○ _____
- ○ _____
- ○ _____
- ○ _____
- ○ _____
- ○ _____

MY *FAITH FOR TODAY* DECLARATION

I will not be discouraged by what I see. I'm standing on what God said!

October
WEEKLY PLANNING

SUNDAY	MONDAY
11	12
	Columbus Day (USA) / Thanksgiving Day (CAN)

TUESDAY	WEDNESDAY
13	14

THURSDAY	FRIDAY
15	16

SATURDAY	*FAITH FOR TODAY* ACTION
17	Share a past victory God gave you — it may stir fresh faith in someone else's heart.

THIS WEEK I SAW GOD WORKING . . .

I'M CELEBRATING . . . OR LOOKING FORWARD TO . . .

October
WEEKLY REFLECTION

NOTES

THIS WEEK'S SCRIPTURE:

"The L/ORD will fight for you; you need only to be still."
EXODUS 14:14

MY PRAYER THIS WEEK:

TO-DO'S:

○ _____
○ _____
○ _____
○ _____
○ _____
○ _____
○ _____
○ _____
○ _____
○ _____

MY *FAITH FOR TODAY* DECLARATION

My breakthrough isn't coming — it's already in motion.
I receive it by faith!

October
WEEKLY PLANNING

SUNDAY	MONDAY
18	19

TUESDAY	WEDNESDAY
20	21

THURSDAY	FRIDAY
22	23

SATURDAY	FAITH FOR TODAY ACTION
24	Stand in faith with someone — pray for their breakthrough like it's your own.

THIS WEEK I SAW GOD WORKING . . .

I'M CELEBRATING . . . OR LOOKING FORWARD TO . . .

October
WEEKLY REFLECTION

NOTES

THIS WEEK'S SCRIPTURE:

Let us not become weary in doing good, for at the proper time we will reap a harvest . . .

GALATIANS 6:9

MY PRAYER THIS WEEK:

TO-DO'S:

- ☐ _____
- ☐ _____
- ☐ _____
- ☐ _____
- ☐ _____
- ☐ _____
- ☐ _____
- ☐ _____
- ☐ _____
- ☐ _____

MY *FAITH FOR TODAY* DECLARATION

I'm walking in strength, favor, and victory. This is my turnaround season, in Jesus' name!

October
WEEKLY PLANNING

SUNDAY	MONDAY
25	26

TUESDAY	WEDNESDAY
27	28

THURSDAY	FRIDAY
29	30

SATURDAY	**FAITH FOR TODAY ACTION**
31	Do something to lighten someone's load this month — a gift, a visit, or a word of life.

Halloween

THIS WEEK I SAW GOD WORKING . . .

I'M CELEBRATING . . . OR LOOKING FORWARD TO . . .

October
WEEKLY REFLECTION

NOTES

When you live with a grateful heart, you shift your focus to all God has given you.

You see His hand in the ordinary. You feel His faithfulness in the details. And you become aware that even in the waiting and hardest places, there's still so much to thank Him for.

No matter what's happening around you, choose to say, "God, I may not have everything I want, but I have all that I need in You." Gratitude opens the door to joy. It silences fear. It softens your heart. And it invites God to do even more in and around you!

Give thanks in all circumstances; for this is God's will for you in Christ Jesus.
1 Thessalonians 5:18

November
AT-A-GLANCE

THIS MONTH, I'M PUTTING MY FAITH IN GOD FOR:

_____
_____
_____
_____
_____

GOALS & DESIRES THIS MONTH:

TO-DO THIS MONTH

- ○ _____
- ○ _____
- ○ _____
- ○ _____
- ○ _____
- ○ _____
- ○ _____

Increase your faith!
Scan now and watch a special message from Pastor Joel!

SUNDAY	MONDAY	TUESDAY	WEDNESDAY
1 Daylight Saving Time ends	2	3	4
8	9	10	11 Veterans Day (USA) / Remembrance Day (CAN)
15	16	17	18
22	23	24	25
29	30	1	2

November

MONTHLY VIEW

THURSDAY	FRIDAY	SATURDAY	NOTES
5	6	7	
12	13	14	
19	20	21	
26 Thanksgiving Day (USA)	27	28	
3	4	5	There is nothing you lack to walk in God's best. — Joel

THIS WEEK'S SCRIPTURE:

Enter his gates with thanksgiving and his courts with praise; give thanks to him and praise his name.

PSALM 100:4

MY PRAYER THIS WEEK:

TO-DO'S:

○ _____
○ _____
○ _____
○ _____
○ _____
○ _____
○ _____
○ _____
○ _____
○ _____

MY *FAITH FOR TODAY* DECLARATION

I am full of gratitude, and I see God's goodness all around me.

November
WEEKLY PLANNING

SUNDAY	MONDAY
1 Daylight Saving Time ends	2
TUESDAY	**WEDNESDAY**
3	4
THURSDAY	**FRIDAY**
5	6
SATURDAY	**FAITH FOR TODAY ACTION**
7	Send a thank-you message to someone who's impacted your life this year.

THIS WEEK I SAW GOD WORKING . . .

I'M CELEBRATING . . . OR LOOKING FORWARD TO . . .

November
WEEKLY REFLECTION

NOTES

THIS WEEK'S SCRIPTURE:

Let the peace of Christ rule in your hearts. . . . And be thankful.

COLOSSIANS 3:15

MY PRAYER THIS WEEK: **TO-DO'S:**

- ○
- ○
- ○
- ○
- ○
- ○
- ○
- ○
- ○
- ○

MY *FAITH FOR TODAY* DECLARATION

Even when things are uncertain, I choose to give thanks — because God is still in control.

November
WEEKLY PLANNING

SUNDAY	MONDAY
8	9

TUESDAY	WEDNESDAY
10	11
	Veterans Day (USA) / Remembrance Day (CAN)

THURSDAY	FRIDAY
12	13

SATURDAY	*FAITH FOR TODAY* ACTION
14	Invite someone over for a meal who might be spending the holidays alone or in need of encouragement.

THIS WEEK I SAW GOD WORKING . . .

I'M CELEBRATING . . . OR LOOKING FORWARD TO . . .

November
WEEKLY REFLECTION

NOTES

THIS WEEK'S SCRIPTURE:

Do not be anxious about anything, but in every situation . . . with thanksgiving, present your requests to God.

PHILIPPIANS 4:6

MY PRAYER THIS WEEK:

TO-DO'S:

- ○ _____
- ○ _____
- ○ _____
- ○ _____
- ○ _____
- ○ _____
- ○ _____
- ○ _____
- ○ _____
- ○ _____

MY *FAITH FOR TODAY* DECLARATION

Gratitude is unlocking greater joy and peace in my life.

November
WEEKLY PLANNING

SUNDAY	MONDAY
15	16

TUESDAY	WEDNESDAY
17	18

THURSDAY	FRIDAY
19	20

SATURDAY	FAITH FOR TODAY ACTION
21	Write handwritten notes of encouragement to your coworkers, teammates, or small group members.

THIS WEEK I SAW GOD WORKING . . .

I'M CELEBRATING . . . OR LOOKING FORWARD TO . . .

November
WEEKLY REFLECTION

NOTES

THIS WEEK'S SCRIPTURE:

Every good and perfect gift is from above, coming down from the Father . . .

JAMES 1:17

MY PRAYER THIS WEEK:

TO-DO'S:

- ○ _____
- ○ _____
- ○ _____
- ○ _____
- ○ _____
- ○ _____
- ○ _____
- ○ _____
- ○ _____
- ○ _____

MY *FAITH FOR TODAY* DECLARATION

Thankfulness will be my song and joy my praise. God has been and always will be worthy of my worship!

November

WEEKLY PLANNING

SUNDAY
22

MONDAY
23

TUESDAY
24

WEDNESDAY
25

THURSDAY
26

Thanksgiving Day (USA)

FRIDAY
27

SATURDAY
28

FAITH FOR TODAY ACTION

Give generously to someone in need — be the answer to their prayer.

THIS WEEK I SAW GOD WORKING . . .

I'M CELEBRATING . . . OR LOOKING FORWARD TO . . .

November
WEEKLY REFLECTION

NOTES

The birth of Jesus is the promise that God sees you, loves you, and is working in your life.

Jesus' arrival means peace in the waiting, strength in the struggle, and light in the darkest places. Because of this, you can celebrate the season with expectation. You can worship with wonder. And, because Jesus came, you have every reason to rejoice.

But the angel said to them, "Do not be afraid. I bring you good news that will cause great joy for all the people."
Luke 2:10

December
AT-A-GLANCE

THIS MONTH, I'M PUTTING MY FAITH IN GOD FOR:

_____
_____
_____
_____
_____
_____

GOALS & DESIRES THIS MONTH:

TO-DO THIS MONTH

- ○ _____
- ○ _____
- ○ _____
- ○ _____
- ○ _____
- ○ _____
- ○ _____

Increase your faith!
Scan now and watch a special message from Pastor Joel!

SUNDAY	MONDAY	TUESDAY	WEDNESDAY
29	30	1	2
6	7	8	9
13	14	15	16
20	21 Winter begins	22	23
27	28	29	30

December
MONTHLY VIEW

THURSDAY	FRIDAY	SATURDAY	NOTES
3	4	5	
10	11	12	
17	18	19	
24 Christmas Eve	25 Christmas Day	26 Boxing Day (CAN)	
31 New Year's Eve	1 New Year's Day	2	Dream big. Pray boldly. Make room for God's abundance! — Joel

THIS WEEK'S SCRIPTURE:

". . . I bring you good news that will cause great joy for all the people."

LUKE 2:10

MY PRAYER THIS WEEK:

TO-DO'S:

- ○
- ○
- ○
- ○
- ○
- ○
- ○
- ○
- ○
- ○

MY *FAITH FOR TODAY* DECLARATION

Because Jesus came, joy lives in me — no matter what's happening around me!

December
WEEKLY PLANNING

SUNDAY	MONDAY
29	30

TUESDAY	WEDNESDAY
1	2

THURSDAY	FRIDAY
3	4

SATURDAY	FAITH FOR TODAY ACTION
5	Spread joy anonymously — leave a note, gift card, or treat for someone who needs encouragement.

THIS WEEK I SAW GOD WORKING . . .

I'M CELEBRATING . . . OR LOOKING FORWARD TO . . .

December
WEEKLY REFLECTION

NOTES

THIS WEEK'S SCRIPTURE:

With joy you will draw water from the wells of salvation.
ISAIAH 12:3

MY PRAYER THIS WEEK:

TO-DO'S:

- ○
- ○
- ○
- ○
- ○
- ○
- ○
- ○
- ○
- ○

MY *FAITH FOR TODAY* DECLARATION

I won't let stress steal my joy. I choose Christ's peace and presence over pressure.

December
WEEKLY PLANNING

SUNDAY 6	MONDAY 7
TUESDAY 8	**WEDNESDAY** 9
THURSDAY 10	**FRIDAY** 11
SATURDAY 12	**FAITH FOR TODAY ACTION**
	Give generously — not just financially, but with your time, words, and attention. Joy multiplies when it's shared.

THIS WEEK I SAW GOD WORKING . . .

I'M CELEBRATING . . . OR LOOKING FORWARD TO . . .

December
WEEKLY REFLECTION

NOTES

THIS WEEK'S SCRIPTURE:

For to us a child is born, to us a son is given, and the government will be on his shoulders. And he will be called Wonderful Counselor, Mighty God, Everlasting Father, Prince of Peace.

ISAIAH 9:6

MY PRAYER THIS WEEK:

TO-DO'S:

- ○ _____
- ○ _____
- ○ _____
- ○ _____
- ○ _____
- ○ _____
- ○ _____
- ○ _____
- ○ _____
- ○ _____

MY *FAITH FOR TODAY* DECLARATION

God's promises are coming to pass. I rejoice in what He's done — and what He's still doing.

December
WEEKLY PLANNING

SUNDAY 13	MONDAY 14
TUESDAY 15	WEDNESDAY 16
THURSDAY 17	FRIDAY 18
SATURDAY 19	**FAITH FOR TODAY ACTION** Volunteer with a local Christmas outreach — help bring joy to someone's holiday.

THIS WEEK I SAW GOD WORKING . . .

I'M CELEBRATING . . . OR LOOKING FORWARD TO . . .

December
WEEKLY REFLECTION

NOTES

THIS WEEK'S SCRIPTURE:

"I have told you this so that my joy may be in you and that your joy may be complete."

JOHN 15:11

MY PRAYER THIS WEEK: **TO-DO'S:**

- ◯
- ◯
- ◯
- ◯
- ◯
- ◯
- ◯
- ◯
- ◯
- ◯

MY *FAITH FOR TODAY* DECLARATION

This season, I'm not just going through the motions.
I'm walking in wonder and worship.

December
WEEKLY PLANNING

SUNDAY
20

MONDAY
21

Winter begins

TUESDAY
22

WEDNESDAY
23

THURSDAY
24

FRIDAY
25

Christmas Eve

Christmas Day

SATURDAY
26

FAITH FOR TODAY ACTION
Text or call someone you haven't talked to in a while — your voice might lift their spirit more than you know.

Boxing Day (CAN)

THIS WEEK I SAW GOD WORKING . . .

I'M CELEBRATING . . . OR LOOKING FORWARD TO . . .

December
WEEKLY REFLECTION

NOTES

THIS WEEK'S SCRIPTURE:

You make known to me the path of life; you will fill me with joy in your presence . . .

PSALM 16:11

MY PRAYER THIS WEEK:

TO-DO'S:

- ○
- ○
- ○
- ○
- ○
- ○
- ○
- ○
- ○
- ○

MY *FAITH FOR TODAY* DECLARATION

The joy of the Lord is my strength — this week and in every season.

December
WEEKLY PLANNING

SUNDAY	MONDAY
27	28

TUESDAY	WEDNESDAY
29	30

THURSDAY	FRIDAY
31	1
New Year's Eve	New Year's Day

SATURDAY	*FAITH FOR TODAY* ACTION
2	Start a family or friend tradition of joy — share highs from the year and declare joy over the year ahead.

THIS WEEK I SAW GOD WORKING . . .

I'M CELEBRATING . . . OR LOOKING FORWARD TO . . .

December
WEEKLY REFLECTION

NOTES

ABOUT JOEL OSTEEN MINISTRIES

Joel Osteen Ministries, rooted in Houston, Texas, is an extension of the legacy built by John and Dodie Osteen, who founded Lakewood Church in 1959. Originally meeting in a modest feedstore, Lakewood has grown into one of the largest congregations in the U.S., attracting people from all walks of life. John Osteen's leadership touched millions through his television ministry, which reached over 100 countries, and his influence as a pastor's pastor. His wife, Dodie, also played a key role, especially with her testimony of miraculous healing from cancer, which has inspired countless people.

When John passed away in 1999, his son Joel stepped into leadership, despite his background in television production. Joel's transition into senior pastor marked a new era for Lakewood, with the church's global influence expanding significantly. Under Joel's leadership, Lakewood's outreach grew, broadcasting to over 200 million households, and the church became a beacon of hope for millions seeking encouragement and inspiration.

Joel's wife, Victoria, serves alongside him, contributing to the church's leadership and vision. Their daughter, Alexandra, continues the family tradition, leading worship and contributing to Lakewood Music. With a focus on uplifting messages and practical teachings, Joel Osteen Ministries aims to reach new generations, inspiring people worldwide to rise above their challenges and live their best life through faith, hope, and love.

Stay encouraged *and* inspired all through the week.

Download the Joel Osteen Daily Podcast *and* subscribe now *on* YouTube to get the latest videos.

For a full listing, visit **JoelOsteen.com/How-To-Watch**.

SiriusXM · **Apple Podcasts** · **Spotify** · **YouTube** · **ROKU**

Stay connected, *be* blessed.

Get more from Joel & Victoria Osteen

It's time to step into the life of victory and favor that God has planned for you! Featuring new messages from Joel & Victoria Osteen, their free daily devotional, and inspiring articles, hope is always at your fingertips with the free Joel Osteen app and online at JoelOsteen.com.

Get the app and visit us today at JoelOsteen.com.

Download on the App Store | GET IT ON Google Play

JOEL OSTEEN MINISTRIES

CONNECT WITH US